The Grace to Desire It

The Grace To Desire It

Meditations on St Benedict's Twelve Degrees of Humility

Dom Pius Mary Noonan, O.S.B.

CANA PRESS

Quotations from the Rule of St Benedict are taken from Abbot Justin McCann's version. Used with permission. Quotations from Holy Scripture are taken from the Douay Rheims Version with the exception of those within Abbot McCann's translation.

CANA PRESS © 2020

Cover image
Praying Monk, William J Forsyth
Courtesy of Indianapolis Museum of Art

For information, address:
PO Box 85
Colebrook,
Tasmania, 7027,
Australia

notredamemonastery.org

ISBN
978-0-6488688-2-8

Humility is nothing but truth, and pride is nothing but lying.

St. Vincent de Paul

Humility, that low, sweet root, from which all heavenly virtues shoot.

St Thomas More

Contents

Preface   ix
Prologue   3
First Degree   7
Second Degree   13
Third Degree   17
Fourth Degree   21
Fifth Degree   27
Sixth Degree   33
Seventh Degree   37
Eighth Degree   43
Ninth Degree   49
Tenth Degree   55
Eleventh Degree   61
Twelfth Degree   67
Conclusion   73
Appendix   77
Prayers for Humility   77

These reflections on the degrees of humility are a collection of thoughts given in the course of the monthly newsletter of Notre Dame Priory. They have been slightly edited here, but they have retained their simple, familial, somewhat direct style. There is no pretension whatsoever to an exegetical commentary on the text, but only a profound desire to help souls who are sincerely striving to progress towards God to discover, in the teachings of St Benedict and the examples of other saints, the gems of holiness that God Himself has sown there, in the pure soul of the Patriarch of Monks.

Dom Pius Mary Noonan, O.S.B.
Notre Dame Priory
Colebrook, Tasmania
21 March 2020, Passing of St Benedict

Rule of St Benedict
Chapter 7
Of humility

Prologue

HOLY Scripture crieth out to us, brethren, saying: *Everyone that exalteth himself shall be humbled, and he that humbleth himself shall be exalted* (Lk 14:11). When it so speaks, it teaches us that all exaltation is a kind of pride; which the prophet shows that he has shunned in the words: *Lord, my heart is not exalted nor mine eyes lifted up; neither have I dwelt on high things, nor on marvels that are beyond my reach* (Ps 130:1). And why? *If I was not humbly minded but exalted my soul with pride; as a child that is weaned from his mother, so wilt thou requite my soul* (Ps 130:2-3).

Wherefore, brethren, if we wish to attain to the summit of humility and desire to arrive speedily at that heavenly exaltation to which we ascend by the humility of the present life, then must we set up a ladder of our ascending actions like unto that which Jacob saw in his vision, whereon angels appeared to him, descending and ascending (cf. Gen 28:12). By that descent and ascent we must surely understand nothing else than this, that we descend by self-exaltation and ascend by humility. And the ladder erected is our life in this world, which for the humble of heart is raised up by the Lord unto heaven. Now the sides of this ladder are our body and soul, into which sides our divine vocation has fitted various degrees of humility and discipline which we have to climb.

There is no such thing as standstill in life. At every moment, we are either growing or fading, rising or falling, progressing or regressing. This is true in the natural as in the supernatural life, but the dynamics are different. Nature seeks to grow, to rise, to develop strength, to take control, to dominate. In the life of grace, we are also meant to do those things, but since we are not, by nature, capable of doing them, and are entirely dependent on divine grace, the measure of our abandonment to God and our reliance on Him is going to be the measure of our progress. In the spiritual life, we rise by descending in the opinion we have of ourselves and by seeking to disappear in the eyes of others, for then we become great in the eyes of God.

Whoever exalts himself is humbled, and whoever humbles himself is exalted. It's as simple as a ladder. Jacob saw the ladder in his sleep, the angels going up and coming down. St Benedict sees here the illustration of what Our Lord would tell us: If we want to rise to God, we must lower ourselves into the abyss of our nothingness. Why is that? Because that is the truth. We are nothing, we have nothing, we can do nothing. *Without me you can do nothing*, Our Lord tells us with the greatest possible clarity (Jn 15:5).

The sides of this ladder are our body and soul, that is to say, our whole composite being placed in this world. Body and soul were made for each other. Both are essential to a human being. Both either go to God, or distance themselves from Him. It is not possible for our soul to be with God if our body does not respect His Law. It is not possible for our body to be pleasing to God even if it performs external works of piety, if our soul is not in communion with Him through faith and love. St Paul made this clear to the Corinthians: *We must all be manifested before the judgment seat of Christ, that every one may receive the proper things of the body, according as he hath done, whether it be good or evil* (2 Cor 5:10). At the end we shall be judged upon the way we lived, upon the movements of our heart and the actions of our body. We have the tools to love and serve God, but, like any tool, they can be misused and turned against their Maker.

St Benedict seeks in the following pages to help us understand why this virtue of humility is so fundamentally important, why it is the foundational virtue upon which one must build one's interior life, and in so doing, he also makes clear that any other foundation will lead to collapse. Any spirituality that is not based on authentic humility and does not put all its trust in God, is only a form of pride, and if we climb that ladder, we will find ourselves at the bottom of the abyss of hell, whereas if we strive to go down in our esteem and in that of others, we will find when we reach the last rung of the ladder, that we have actually risen to the greatest heights. And so it is clear that humility is not only for monks.

So let's get going. Remember, we are going *down*.

First Degree

The first degree of humility, then, is that a man keep *the fear of God before his eyes* (Ps 35:2), altogether shunning forgetfulness. Let him ever remember all the commandments of God and how hell will burn for their sins those that despise Him; and let him constantly turn over in his heart the eternal life which is prepared for those that fear Him. And guarding himself always from sins and vices, whether of thought, word, hand, foot or self-will, and checking also the desires of the flesh, let him consider that God is always beholding him from heaven, that his actions are everywhere visible to the eye of the Godhead, and are constantly being reported to God by the angels. The prophet teaches us when he represents God as always present in our thoughts: *God searcheth the heart and the reins* (Ps 7:10). And again: *The Lord knoweth the thoughts of men* (Ps 93:11). And again he saith: *Thou hast understood my thoughts from afar* (Ps 138:3); and: *The thought of man shall praise thee* (Ps 75:11). In order then that he may be careful regarding his wrongful thoughts, let the good brother say constantly in his heart: *Then shall I be spotless before him, if I shall have kept myself from my iniquity* (Ps 17:24).

We are, indeed, forbidden to do our own will by Scripture, which saith to us: *Turn away from thine own will* (Sir 18:30). Moreover, we ask God in prayer that *His will be done* (Mt 6:10) in us. And rightly are we taught not to do our own will, since we dread that sentence of Scripture: *There are ways which to men seem right, but the ends thereof lead to the depths of hell* (Prov 16:25); and since we fear also what is said of the careless: *They are corrupt and have become abominable in their (pleasures)* (Ps 13:1). And in regard to the desires of the flesh, let us believe that God is always present to us, since the prophet says to the Lord: *All my desire is before thee* (Ps 37:10).

We must be on our guard, then, against evil desires, for death lies close by the gate of delight; whence Scripture gives this command: *Go not after thy lusts* (Sir 18:30). So if the *eyes of the Lord behold the good and the evil* (Prov 15:3), and the Lord is *ever looking down from heaven upon the children of men, to see if there be one soul that reflects and seeks God* (Ps 13:2); and if our deeds are daily, day and night, reported to the Lord by the angels assigned to us: then, brethren, must we constantly beware, as the prophet says in the Psalm, lest God some day behold us falling into evil ways, and *turned unprofitable* (Ps 13:3), and spare us for this present time, because He is merciful and awaits our amendment, but should say to us in the future: *These things didst thou do, and I was silent* (Ps 49:20).

St Benedict loved the psalms; no less than nine of them are quoted in this first degree of humility — just to say how important the psalms are in our lives—; the text is a nearly inexhaustible source of meditation. We can safely summarise it this way: "Always keep God before your eyes, never forget the four last things: death, judgment, heaven and hell." What a powerful insight and a penetrating maxim! Perhaps the most fundamental words to consign to memory are: *altogether shunning forgetfulness.* Forgetfulness is one of the most dangerous plagues of the spiritual life: we tend to forget eternal realities because we do not see them, and we get ourselves involved with worldly things because we do see them. *Altogether shunning forgetfulness.* Remember who you are, where you came from, where you are going, why you are here. Ask yourself often what God thinks of you, how He considers this particular action you are engaged in or about to do; how does He like this thought you have on your mind and which you like to dwell upon; how does it fit in with His eternal law, which will never change and by which you must be guided if you do not wish to destroy yourself?

The mention of the angels continually going back and forward between God and us, reporting everything to Him, should put us on our guard — it is destined to keep us in line —, but it is also a great consolation: my Guardian Angel is continually going to God to report on my activities, but He is also bringing God's grace to do good and avoid evil. He is my best friend, and if I listen to his sweet voice, I shall live a good life and be saved. Never forget that he is your ally in the battle against the forces of evil and that he is stronger than all the forces of hell put together for the simple reason that he is on God's side; sadden him not by sin, but give him the joy of seeing your progress each day in virtue and in holiness. One day you will see him face to face and thank him for his lifelong fidelity.

All this, my dear Friend, is matter for lengthy meditation and prayer, and will, I hope, nourish yours for many days to come. Remember: shun forgetfulness! So many get nowhere because they are spiritually absent-minded. Keep on the ball, every day of your life, by means of your daily meditation.

There is an interesting parallel to make here with the degrees of humility as presented by St Ignatius of Loyola in the Spiritual Exercises. For him, the first degree of humility, which is necessary for salvation, "consists in this, that as far as possible I so subject and humble myself as to obey the law of God our Lord in all things, so that not even were I made lord of all creation, or to save my life here on earth, would I consent to violate a commandment, whether divine or human, that binds me under pain of mortal sin" (*Sp. Ex.* #165).

For Ignatius, the minimum humility required is to avoid mortal sin. Sin, every sin, involves a degree of pride. It implies, at least implicitly, not accepting God's law, not respecting the nature He has given us, and wanting to make our own rules, which we consider to be sovereign, at least at the moment we give in to sin. Ultimately, every sin is a form of idolatry: it makes the individual the supreme rule and the only source of morality. This is all the more important in an age where there is an increasing tendency to give to the individual conscience the autonomy to decide what is good and evil. Is that not the essence of the very first temptation in the

Garden of Eden: "If you eat that fruit, you shall be as gods, knowing what is good and evil" (cf. Gen 3:5)— "knowing", meaning "deciding for yourself"?

So, to avoid mortal sin, one must subject oneself to obey the law of God — in all things. Question: Do we often look at it that way? Do we consider, when we are in the grip of temptation, that our salvation depends on whether or not we have enough humility to not offend God? We all experience moments of temptation, when it would be so easy to give into an impulse without anyone knowing it and possibly without any foreseeable bad consequences. But the real question we must ask ourselves is: am I violating a serious command of God? If I am, I am showing my pride, I am obeying Satan rather than God, and I am doing something that will jeopardise my eternal salvation. It's so very important to keep this in mind: a mortal sin, as a serious offence against the Divine Law, is *humanly* irreparable. What that means is that man has no power in himself to make up for it. Just as you cannot lift yourself up by the lobes of your own ears or by the straps of your own boots, you cannot bring yourself back to the life of grace once it has been lost. Only God can do that. He does so through the sacrament of Penance, but that sacrament is not a given, not something we have at our disposal as a fundamental right that we can demand of God; it remains a free gift on His part, and it requires of us the humility of acknowledging our transgression, accepting to do penance and resolving not to sin again. The humility we did not have and the lack of which led us to sin, we must obtain in order to confess our sin.

So the point we must always keep in mind in times of temptation is: do I accept being in an order of things that

I did not make, that does not depend on my personal pref-erences, but is determined by the omnipotent Creator and provident Father of the universe? If I do not, I place myself outside of that order, and I lose all the benefits of it. If I do, then I have the beginnings of humility.

Second Degree

The second degree of humility is that a man love not his own will, nor delight in fulfilling his own desires, but carry out in deed the saying of the Lord: I *came not to do my own will, but the will of Him who sent me* (Jn 6:38). It is written also: 'Self-will hath its punishment, but necessity winneth a crown'.

"Be on guard against your own will": a counter-cultural affirmation if there ever was one! I suspect that most of our contemporaries would not have a clue as to what it means. In our day, the will of the individual is supreme: "do *your* thing"; "all that matters is what *you* want"; "it's all about *you*"... Don't we hear such expressions every day? So how can we understand this teaching? Does it really make sense, and if so, how?

I suggest that we first need to do a bit of philosophy. Man is a limited, finite creature, endowed with intellect and free will. This will is, by nature, oriented towards and drawn by the good, since it is ultimately destined to be appeased with the possession of the absolute Good which is God. But everything that exists is, in some way, good; otherwise it would not exist. In this life, the intellect often perceives only a partial good and fails to see its evil consequences; likewise, the lower faculties of man are drawn to particular goods that are sometimes in contradiction with reason, and this attraction inclines the will to pursue these apparent goods which, in reality, cannot fulfil the purpose of his existence, but will only leave him empty and lead to his destruction and damnation.

This was true of our first parents in the state of original justice, and that is why they sinned. But it is even more true of us, due to the fact that we are born with concupiscence (the attraction to sensual pleasures contrary to reason) and ignorance (a darkness of the intellect making it difficult to see where the true good lies).

This is why St Benedict insists upon the necessity to not follow one's own will. One's own will always runs the risk of pursuing a particular good and of leaving aside the general and ultimate good of our nature. The only way to prevent this from happening is to discipline oneself to ensure the rectitude of the intellect and will, and the safest and easiest way to do this is to follow the ordinances laid down by an authority that speaks to us in God's name. And that is the reason for which every authentic pursuit of God passes through the mediation of a creature, the supreme form of mediation being the Church.

But if this is so, then someone who is advanced and has a solid spiritual life would be able to do their own will, because they have become accustomed to doing what is good, right? Not always, says St Benedict, backed by Holy Scripture: *There is a way that seemeth to a man right: and the ends thereof lead to death* (Pr 16:25). Many have been led astray by following their own light, resorting to their own devices in the spiritual life. Whereas the saints tell us that even *they* need a spiritual guide and someone to obey, the evil spirit tries to persuade souls to be self-sufficient, to forge their own way to God ("I did it my way"…) ; for this is precisely what he tried to do: he wanted to be like God in *his* way, he refused to acknowledge the limits of his own created intellect, and imagined he could climb to the throne of God by relying on *his own* strength. In the end, that is the very essence of every sin.

And that is why, as St Benedict says: "we ask God in prayer that His will be done in us", which is, of course, a reference to the Our Father in which we pray: *Thy will be done on earth as it is in Heaven.* But when we recite the Lord's Prayer, we insist not so much on not doing our will as on doing God's will. Here too, we need to pause for a moment: what's so great about doing somebody else's will? Many would argue today that it is much more fulfilling to do one's own will than that of another. And yet, even in human society we can readily perceive that this is not always a good thing. Many people would acknowledge that, for the sake of peace and harmony, it is better to accept someone else's way of doing things, at least in certain areas. That is not at all what we are talking about here. When we say *Thy will be done,* we are speaking to the Eternal Creator whose will is, always, everywhere and in all things, perfect and ideal. Whatever God wills is, by its very nature and simply because He wills it, not only good, but best for all involved. God has an infinitely good plan for each of us, and if we followed that plan and lived it to the full, then the world would be an exceedingly happy place to live, in which everyone would be perfectly happy and content, for all would be concurring together to the good of the whole: the Creator would be glorified, and the creature fulfilled beyond his wildest dreams.

But few are those who understand this and accept its discipline, and that is why the world is a mess... May our holy Father St Benedict and all the saints intercede for us and help us to realise this in our daily lives.

Third Degree

The third degree of humility is that a man for the love of God subject himself to his superior in all obedience, imitating the Lord, of whom the apostle says: *He was made obedient even unto death* (Ph 2:8).

Not to love one's own will; not to delight in fulfilling one's own desires; to be content to do someone else's will; to find satisfaction in submitting's one's thoughts and desires to someone whose role it is to guide us. Not exactly fashionable! There is only one way to understand the value of these attitudes, and that is faith in the Lord Jesus Christ, utter confidence in the knowledge that the way He lived is the best way, the one that will profit us most for eternal salvation and perfection.

Christian perfection in fact lies in the imitation of the God-Man, Jesus Christ. Now, it is an aspect of His life that He consistently portrays himself as having come to obey. This is utterly astounding. If anyone was ever in a position to do his own will without the worry of it not being in conformity with the Divine Will, it was Our Lord. His human will was so perfectly in unison with His Divine Will that there was no possibility of any lack of fidelity to God and the demands of the perfect life. Nevertheless, He tells us He comes not to do His own, that is to say *human* will, but that of the Father. He will even go so far as to say: *My food is to do the will of Him who sent me* (Jn 4:34). My *food*, that is to say, what nourishes me and keeps me moving. In other words, I just can't live without doing the will of my Father; I would accomplish it at any cost. Far from perceiving His role as one of self-affirmation, it is as if the Lord wants to efface Himself before the will of the Father. *I do always the things that please Him* (Jn 8:29) — what love of the Son for the Father, what fascination for Him!

The Son knows the Father perfectly, being the expression of all that He is; He loves Him eternally as God. But His created human soul is so enamoured of the beauty of the Father that all He wants to do is fulfill His will, even though He knows that this will is going to have very high demands on Him, for it will lead to the Cross. As He reaches the end of His life, just before expiring, He says: *It is consummated* (Jn 19:30), and St John points out that these words reflect Our Lord's great desire to fufill the prophecies concerning Him. He simply could not die until He had fulfilled each and every one, down to the last minute detail.

And this was the case from the very moment of the Incarnation. The Epistle to the Hebrews tells us, quoting Psalm 39: *Sacrifice and oblation Thou wouldst not: but a body Thou hast fitted to me. Holocausts for sin did not please Thee. Then said I: Behold I come: in the head of the book it is written of me:*

that I should do Thy will, O God (Heb 10:5-7). These words were recited by Our Lord; they were in His Heart even as He entered this world.

The lesson we can draw from this is that no number of great works – prayers, fastings, sacrifices of any sort – are of any value whatsoever if they are the expression of self-will. All our sanctification lies not in conceiving and realising great plans that we imagine will be pleasing to God, but in embracing the Divine Will, in doing the will of the Other, the Eternal Other who has brought us into existence and in Whom Alone our life finds meaning and purpose.

Even though Our Lord brings this attitude to its perfection, it had already been taught in the Old Testament. When King Saul thought he was doing something praiseworthy by offering only the first-fruits to God of the spoils of the Amalekites instead of offering everything as the Lord had commanded, he was told by the prophet Samuel: *Doth the Lord desire holocausts and victims, and not rather that the voice of the Lord should be obeyed? For obedience is better than sacrifices: and to hearken rather than to offer the fat of rams. Because it is like the sin of witchcraft, to rebel: and like the crime of idolatry, to refuse to obey. Forasmuch, therefore, as thou hast rejected the word of the Lord, the Lord hath also rejected thee from being king* (1 Sam 15:22-23).

It is good for us to keep this in mind when we are inclined to do anything for God. We need to ask ourselves: is this really what God wants for me, or is it my own ego that is fooling me into thinking it is so? The way to resolve this dilemma is humility. A truly humble soul will always question itself on its deepest motivations and intentions; it will always be on its guard against self-will, for it knows that it can easily be led astray, and that by obeying, by submitting oneself to the guidance of another who commands in God's stead, one avoids the risk of departing from the path of salvation.

If this attitude is one of humility, it is also one of love, for humility both leads to love and proceeds from it. It leads to it because when you have come to realise your own nothingness and how much you have received from God, you feel moved to love Him more. It proceeds from it, for once charity begins to grow in the soul, it deepens further the love we have for the Beloved. It is proper for the lover to want to lower himself under the beloved, as St Therese of Lisieux said so beautifully. This is perhaps what Our Lord tried to get across to His disciples when He said at the Last Supper: *That the world may know that I love the Father: and as the Father hath given me commandment, so do I. Arise, let us go hence* (Jn 14:31).

In conclusion, let us read the words with which St Alphonsus Liguori opens his marvellous little work on *Uniformity with God's Will*. He writes: "Perfection is founded entirely on the love of God: *Charity is the bond of perfection* (Col 3:14) and perfect love of God means the complete union of our will with God's: the principal effect of love is so to unite the wills of those who love each other as to make them will the same things. It follows then, that the more one unites his will with the divine will, the greater will be his love of God".

Fourth Degree

The fourth degree of humility is that, meeting in this obedience with difficulties and contradictions and even injustice, he should with a silent mind hold fast to patience, and enduring neither tire nor run away, for the Scripture saith: *He that shall persevere to the end shall be saved* (Mt 10:22); and again: *Let thy heart take courage, and wait thou for the Lord* (Ps 26:14). And showing how the true disciple ought to endure all things, however contrary, for the Lord, it saith in the person of sufferers: *For thy sake we face death at every moment. We are reckoned no better than sheep marked down for slaughter* (Rom 8:36; Ps 43:22). Then, confident in their hope of the divine reward, they go on with joy to declare: *But in all these things we overcome, through Him that hath loved us* (Rom 8:38). And again in another place the Scripture saith: *Thou, O God, hast put us to the proof: Thou hast tested us as men test silver in the fire. Thou hast led us into a snare: Thou hast bowed our backs with trouble* (Ps 65:11). And to show that we ought to be under a superior, it goeth on to say: *Thou hast set men over our heads* (Ps 65:12). Moreover, in adversities and injuries they patiently fulfil the Lord's commands: when struck on one cheek they offer the other, when robbed of their tunic they surrender also their cloak, when forced to go a mile they go two (cf. Mt 5:39-41), with the apostle Paul they bear with false brethren, and they bless those that curse them (cf. 2 Cor 11:26; 1 Cor 4:12).

The steps to humility outlined by St Benedict are not necessarily intended to describe a chronological ascent, and that is why commentators have various ways of grouping them together. One is to consider the first four degrees as a summary of the entire monastic life. In the first, we learn the saving fear of God and live in His presence; in the second we live not by our own will but that of the Lord; in the third, we go further in accepting that God's will is made known to us, not directly as a matter of course, but by human mediation, especially that of our superiors. Here, in the fourth degree, when one meets with all the hardship that the life of obedience involves, one is content with things being that way; one does not run away, but bears with it, confident that this is the path to true happiness in this life and the next. There can be little doubt that this degree is in many ways a summit.

When one reads the text, there are many episodes from the lives of saints that come to mind because they illustrate it so perfectly, the martyrs in particular. These great saints exercised in the most sublime way the virtue of fortitude, the first act of which is to bear up under suffering and persecution. They did not run away, they endured the pain and the scorn, because their heart was strengthened interiorly by Divine Grace. In the eyes of men, they seemed to be overcome, but in reality, they were the ones who were victorious. In this, they did only imitate Our Blessed Lord, whom His enemies taunted while He hung on the cross. They challenged Him to come down from the cross to show His power. But in reality, the most striking and inspiring manifestation of his power was actually staying on the cross, and enduring the mockery and torment.

We may also call to mind the "perfect joy of St Francis", that touching scene in the life of the Poverello where he is walking in cold rain from Perugia to Saint Mary of the Angels, in company with Brother Leo, suffering greatly from the cold. St Francis calls to his companion: "Br Leo, if it were to please God that the Friars Minor should give, in all lands, a great example of holiness and edification, write down, and note carefully, that this would not be perfect joy."

A little further on, St Francis called to him a second time: "O Br Leo, if the Friars Minor were to make the lame to walk, if they should make straight the crooked, chase away demons, give sight to the blind, hearing to the deaf, speech to the dumb, and, what is even a far greater work, if they should raise the dead after four days, write that this would not be perfect joy."

After walking on for a little while, he cried out again: "O Br Leo, if the Friars Minor knew all languages; if they were versed in all science; if they could explain all Scripture; if they had the gift of prophecy, and could reveal, not only all future things, but likewise the secrets of all consciences and all souls, write that this would not be perfect joy."

Proceeding a few steps farther, he called out again with a loud voice: "O Br Leo, thou little lamb of God! if the Friars Minor could speak with the tongues of angels; if they could explain the course of the stars; if they knew the virtues of all plants; if all the treasures of the earth were revealed to them; if they were acquainted with the various qualities of all birds, of all fish, of all animals, of men, of trees, of stones, of roots, and of waters — write that this would not be perfect joy."

A bit further on, he once again exclaimed: "O Br Leo, if the Friars Minor had the gift of preaching so as to convert all infidels to the faith of Christ, write that this would not be perfect joy."

Br Leo, as you might imagine, was quite intrigued by all this and was wondering greatly where it was leading. When he had gone on for the space of two miles, he mustered up the courage to question the saint: "Father, I pray thee teach me wherein is perfect joy." St Francis answered: "If, when we shall arrive at Saint Mary of the Angels, all drenched with rain and trembling with cold, all covered with mud and exhausted from hunger; if, when we knock at the convent-gate, the porter should come angrily and ask us who we are; if, after we have told him, 'We are two of the brethren', he should answer angrily, 'What ye say is not the truth; ye are but two impostors going about to deceive the world and take away the alms of the poor; begone I say'; if then he refuse to open to us, and leave us outside, exposed to the snow and rain, suffering from cold and hunger till nightfall — then, if we accept such injustice, such cruelty and such contempt with patience, without being ruffled and without murmuring, believing with humility and charity that the porter really knows us, and that it is God who maketh him

to speak thus against us, write down, O Br Leo, that this is perfect joy.

"And if we knock again, and the porter come out in anger to drive us away with oaths and blows, as if we were vile impostors, saying, 'Begone, miserable robbers, to the hospital, for here you shall neither eat nor sleep!' — and if we accept all this with patience, with joy, and with charity, O Br Leo, write that this indeed is perfect joy.

"And if, urged by cold and hunger, we knock again, calling to the porter and entreating him with many tears to open to us and give us shelter, for the love of God, and if he come out more angry than before, exclaiming, 'These are but importunate rascals, I will deal with them as they deserve'; and taking a knotted stick, he seize us by the hood, throwing us on the ground, rolling us in the snow, and shall beat and wound us with the knots in the stick — if we bear all these injuries with patience and joy, thinking of the sufferings of our Blessed Lord, which we would share out of love for him, write, O Brother Leo, that here, finally, is perfect joy.

"And now, Brother, listen to the conclusion. Above all the graces and all the gifts of the Holy Ghost which Christ grants to His friends, is the grace of overcoming oneself, and accepting willingly, out of love for Christ, all suffering, injury, discomfort and contempt; for in all other gifts of God we cannot glory, seeing they proceed not from ourselves but from God, according to the words of the Apostle, *What hast thou that thou hast not received from God? and if thou hast received it, why dost thou glory as if thou hadst not received it?* (1 Cor 4:7). But in the cross of tribulation and affliction we may glory, because, as the Apostle says again, *I will not glory save in the cross of our Lord Jesus Christ* (Gal 6:14). Amen."

And in those last words lies the secret of St Benedict, of St Francis and of all the saints; therein lies the secret of religious life with its trials and humiliations; there too is found the secret of the fidelity of so many spouses who, in spite of injustice, remain true to their word; there is the secret of the martyrs, rejoicing as they are led to death. There, finally, is the secret that led St Ignatius to have his retreatant not only esteem humiliations, but to actually ask God for the grace to be favoured with them (cf. Sp. Ex. # 98, 147, 157, 167). Our glory is indeed in the cross of our Lord Jesus Christ. *For me to live is Christ and to die is gain* (Ph 1:21).

Fifth Degree

The fifth degree of humility is that he humbly confess and conceal not from his abbot any evil thoughts that enter his heart, and any secret sins that he has committed. To this does Scripture exhort us, saying: *Make known thy way unto the Lord and hope in Him* (Ps 36:5). And again: *Confess to the Lord, for He is good, and His mercy endureth for ever* (Ps 105:1). And further: *I have made known my sin to Thee, and my faults I have not concealed. I said: I will be my own accuser and confess my faults to the Lord, and with that Thou didst remit the guilt of my sin* (Ps 31:5).

St Benedict here refers to a commonplace teaching among all Catholic spiritual masters, which we could summarise in these words: you can't do it alone. We might begin by drawing a comparison with the human realms of any knowledge or skill. No one can master an art on his own. He needs the guidance of others who have been there before him and can teach him aspects of the question he does not suspect, or which it would take him a very long time to figure out on his own. Life is so complex and so short, that the person who wants to do it all on his own will get virtually nothing done. Life is not to be reinvented every time someone comes into the world. Why is it then that one could imagine being able to progress in the *spiritual* life without a guide? The realm of the mind and heart is infinitely more complex than any natural science or realm of study, for it deals with the subtlest movements of the heart and, more importantly, is destined to lead to the contemplation of the eternal God, infinitely removed from our capacity to comprehend.

God has put us in this life to seek Him, find Him, and ultimately climb the steep path to His heavenly abode where we hope to see Him face to face. Impossible, indeed, if we had to achieve it on our own. That is precisely why God stepped into our world, to guide us to Himself. He gave us a Church to whom He has entrusted the task of speaking in His Name the saving doctrine and showing us the path to Heaven. This is why those who wish to be among the Lord's intimates and for whom the interior life of the soul is truly the most valuable part of life, they, more than anyone else, need a guide. For the way is narrow (cf. Mt 7:14), it is steep, it is lined with traps and dangers. St John of the Cross says that when the soul has reached a certain level of union with God, the path disappears, you no longer know where you are, you are in the dark night of faith. Then, if you have no guide, you will be lost.

Such is the background of St Benedict's teaching on the humility which moves the monk to admit to his abbot all his failings. Without such a confession, it would be impossible to progress in the interior life. Mind you, the confession to the abbot here described is not sacramental confession. That is another realm, directly related to the power of the keys held by the Church in the person of her priests. Any priest can forgive, in the sacrament of penance, the sins we have committed. Here, St Benedict is referring to the openness that takes place in the context of spiritual direction. The soul opens itself up like a book to an experienced spiritual mentor who knows the ways of the Spirit and can be a trusted and sure guide.

St Ignatius of Loyola concurs when, in the 17th annotation, he admonishes the director of the Spiritual Exercises not to pry into the secret thoughts of the retreatant, but adds that "it will be very helpful if he is kept faithfully informed about the various disturbances and thoughts caused by the action of different spirits. This will enable him to propose some spiritual exercises in accordance with the degree of progress made and suited and adapted to the needs of a soul disturbed in this way" (*Sp. Ex.* # 17). The spiritual director is unable to give sound advice of discernment unless he knows what is going on in the heart of the retreatant; the great importance of spiritual openness is evident.

St Ignatius returns to this in more depth in the 13th rule for discernment of spirits: "Our enemy may also be compared in his manner of acting to a false lover. He seeks to remain hidden and does not want to be discovered. If such a lover speaks with evil intention to the daughter of a good father, or to the wife of a good husband, and seeks to seduce them, he wants his words and solicitations kept secret. He is greatly displeased if his evil suggestions and depraved intentions are revealed by the daughter to her father, or by the wife to her husband. Then he readily sees he will not succeed in what he has begun. In the same way, when the enemy of our human nature tempts a just soul with his wiles and seductions, he earnestly desires that they be received secretly and kept secret. But if one manifests them to a confessor, or to some other spiritual person who understands his deceits and malicious designs, the evil one is very much vexed. For he knows that he cannot succeed in his evil undertaking, once his evident deceits have been revealed" (*Sp. Ex. #* 326).

How often has experience shown that by manifesting one's temptations to a trustworthy person, they disappear on the spot! Spiritual solitude is dangerous, for the devil is cunning, and he is evil. If we manifest our failings and bad thoughts to a wise person, the enemy loses power over us. Moreover, there is a psychological reason for this: by manifesting our deepest thoughts, we are no longer alone with them, there is someone else there to help us. However, there is a much deeper reason, and that is humility. If St Benedict places these reflections here, it is because he knows that it takes humility to open the wounds of one's heart to someone else. But he also knows that when the soul finds the courage to open itself up, such openness is going to increase its humility.

There is a famous episode in the life of St Thérèse of Lisieux, which she herself recounts in the *Story of a Soul*. She tells how, the day before her profession, during the hour of silent prayer in choir, she was tormented with the thought that she did not have a vocation, and that she was fooling everyone into thinking she did. The temptation was so obsessive that it seemed clear as day to her that she should not make profession, but should leave the convent. With that she rose, made her way to the the Novice Mistress, asked her to come with her outside, and then proceeded to tell her that she was now sure she had no vocation, that she had been deluding everyone including herself. The Novice Mistress saw through the temptation and reassured her. But Therese wanted to make her act of humility more complete, and revealed the thought to the Prioress also who simply laughed at the young novice – and that was the end of the temptation: the diabolical illusion disappeared with the act of humbly uncovering the terrible thought of the heart.

Remember: if you feel inclined to hide your thoughts because you are ashamed, that is a sure sign that you need to tell a trustworthy person about it. "A fault confessed is half redressed", goes the saying. And a temptation avowed, is more than half conquered.

Sixth Degree

The sixth degree of humility is that a monk be content with the meanest and worst of everything, and esteem himself, in regard to the work that is given him, as a bad and unworthy workman, saying to himself with the prophet: *I am brought to nothing; I am all ignorance; I am become as a dumb beast before thee; yet am I ever close to Thee* (Ps 72:22-23).

We have entered, with this sixth degree of humility, into a zone of even greater misunderstanding with the modern world. It would be difficult to express more acutely the opposite of what the world preaches. In every clime, on every news channel, all over the internet, we see the promotion of self, of personal rights, of ways to make the most money, to get the best merchandise, reap the most praise and applause. It's the ongoing "rat race" to fleeting pleasure, ephemeral beauty, and short-lived power.

As is common with the saints, because they are rooted in the Word of God, St Benedict's remedy simply counteracts the whole idea, strikes it at the root, and deals it the death blow. This he does in two principal ways.

The first is by stressing that the monk is to be content with what is at hand, even if that is the meanest and the worst. The humble person, due to a very modest opinion of himself, is quite happy to have very little, to not be favoured by the best the world has to offer. If you are of the world, if your opinion of yourself is high and mighty, then most likely you will not be satisfied with what comes your way; you will imagine yourself entitled to more, to better, to the best. This attitude is exacerbated in our world which has seen the quasi-disappearance of social classes. In former times, the peasant would never have aspired to the life of the noble; he was usually content with his lot, and if so, he could be quite happy. But nowadays everyone is king and thinks himself entitled to the best. St Benedict's message, re-read today, is countercultural and says something like: it may be that there are no more social divides — and that may be, at least in certain respects, a good thing — but the fact remains that the humble person is content with what comes, even if what comes is pretty lousy. Put simply, humility is the secret to happiness, because it is the secret to accepting things as they are. Pride, on the other hand, is the secret to misery. It can never accept the last place, which often — whether we like it or not — is where we find ourselves.

The second way is to take a long hard look at oneself and then to acknowledge that we are not that flawless person we thought. St Benedict's text might seem hard to stomach: how can one honestly consider oneself a bad workman, when one is good at what one does? Here we need to ward off a false interpretation. Humility is truth, and being humble will never mean going against the truth. If someone happens to be a piano prodigy, that person can hardly think truthfully that they know nothing about the piano. For them, humility consists in acknowledging their gift, but attributing it to the goodness of God. If such a person is truly humble and finds himself, for whatever reason, obliged to undertake less gratifying work such as house-cleaning or dishes, humility helps him to see such work as a grace: the work is not beneath him; he discovers that in it he can improve, and he will consequently strive to perfect himself in it.

But one might object: "St Benedict is here speaking about monks, and he's actually up to the sixth degree, so this is a pretty high degree of humility. Do you honestly think that a successful CEO or a Hollywood star can content themselves with the lowly tasks that in former ages would have been reserved to the lower classes?" I do, and there are two very good reasons for which everyone is capable of becoming truly humble, provided they take time to meditate upon these truths frequently.

The first reason is that we have been created out of nothing by the gratuitous love of God, who continues freely to preserve us in existence: if He did not, we would return to nothingness. This is expressed in another way by saying that the "creature without the Creator vanishes". Fundamentally, each one of us remains utterly dependant upon the Creator, not just for our creation in the maternal womb, but also for our present existence. No one is necessary. No one has a *right* to existence. No one can pretend to be autonomous. Just as our life depends at every moment on the availability of oxygen to breathe, without which we would suffocate and die, so our very being is utterly, ontologically dependent upon the Creator: if He were to forget us for just an instant, we would at that very moment fall back into oblivion, and every trace of our existence would disappear. Spend some time dwelling upon that, and you will find yourself feeling pretty small. And that's a good feeling to have, for you *are* small.

If that's not enough to elicit some profound attitudes of humility, there is a second consideration, namely that there is something in us that is inferior to nothingness itself: the disorder of sin and its effects. As sinners who have turned away from God, who have mocked the very source and origin of our being, we find ourselves spiritually below zero. The contemplation of the eternal punishment of hell for unrepented sin can help a lot towards coming to realise the gravity of sin. But there is also the contemplation of the passion of Our Lord. Jesus died for my sins, He suffered a cruel death for my sins. And if He had not done so, I would be lost. Each one of those points is food for thought whenever we are inclined, foolishly so, to put ourselves over our neighbour, to think we deserve better. Honestly? Have we taken the full measure of our deserts?

Such thoughts should help put us in the right disposition of soul that would make it possible to achieve the sixth degree of humility. When a person is convinced that the world does not revolve around them (it doesn't!), that they are not the centre of the universe (you're not!), that actually many of the problems of the world just might be in some way due to their own sins (they are!), then one can see why it is possible to be content with the "meanest and worst of everything".

Then you find peace, because you have found freedom. You are no longer enslaved by the chimera of illusory grandeur. You can let God be God, and you are then free to play the role of a creature, a very small one — it is true — in the grand scheme of things, but one that becomes great precisely when, and to the degree that, one is convinced of its insignificance.

Seventh Degree

The seventh degree of humility is that he should not only in his speech declare himself lower and of less account than all others, but should in his own inmost heart believe it, humbling himself and saying with the prophet: *But I am a worm and no man, a byword to all men and the laughing-stock of the people* (Ps 21:7). *I have been lifted up only to be humbled and confounded* (Ps 87:16); and again: *It is good for me that Thou hast humbled me: that I may learn Thy commandments* (Ps 118:71).

With this degree of humility, we have reached a still deeper level of the virtue. Whereas in the preceding degrees, one could, conceivably, go through the actions of accepting the outward humiliations — obeying, bearing insults, opening of one's heart to an elder, being given the worst of everything —, but without it necessarily bringing on a deeper sense of conversion, here it is clear that there can no longer be a façade, for all the masks have been thrown off. The monk who has achieved this level will willingly acknowledge that others are better than he, that he is deserving only of hardship and labour, and these words will be the honest expression of what he really feels deep down in his heart.

To highlight his teaching, St Benedict, as is his custom, has recourse to the Psalms, the numerous quotations of which reveal a man who is very familiar with the psalter. This is only to be expected of one who, along with almost the entire western tradition, mandates the recitation of the full psalter every week of the year. Three Psalms are brought in to support the saint's teaching here.

The first is the great Psalm of the Passion, Psalm 21, in which the psalmist saw in a prophetic vision the sufferings of the future Messiah, His rejection by His people, the torments of His passion. As the text puts it, the Christ will be so disfigured that he will appear more as a worm than a man, one upon whom people trample out of scorn. The use St Benedict makes of the verse indicates that the truly humble monk is not only accepting of mistreatment (we saw that exemplified in the fourth degree), but also, in the midst of it, remains at peace because he truly believes in his heart that such is what he deserves.

The second is also a Psalm of the Passion, but it is the one Psalm that has a bad ending. All the other psalms conclude with hope of a future salvation and restoration. Psalm 87 ends in a form of profound desolation: "*Thy wrath hath come upon me: and thy terrors have troubled me. They have come round about me like water all the day: they have compassed me about together. Friend and neighbour thou hast put far from me: and my acquaintance, because of misery*" (Ps 87:17-19). The verse, however, quoted by St Benedict refers to a previous exaltation, and a subsequent humiliation, which seemingly highlights the fact that the monk should grow in a desire for humiliations. Whereas the natural bent of human nature is to increase in the esteem of others, the monk should seek to decrease. If he was once exalted, either because of his birth or his talents or his position before or after he entered the monastery, he wants to eventually be brought down and humiliated, and this is good. It's a paradox, but the more the monk progresses in his monastic life, the more he should want to be and the more he should actually be, humiliated.

The third is the long Psalm 118, which sings the beauties of the Law of the Lord. The particular verse quoted by St Benedict immediately follows a reference to the persecutions suffered at the hands of the wicked who despise God's law: *"The iniquity of the proud hath been multiplied over me: but I will seek Thy commandments with my whole heart. Their heart is curdled like milk: but I have meditated on Thy law"* (Ps 118:69-70). It is as if to say that the monk might very well be brought low in humiliation precisely because of his fidelity to God's law. Even though one would not expect such a thing to happen in a monastery, it can come about that a monk be persecuted for doing good, even by other monks and his superiors. This does not mean, of course, that the superiors and other monks who would inflict such suffering are necessarily ill-intentioned, for sometimes even good souls can be led astray and be under the illusion that it is their duty to persecute a very good and God-fearing confrere. God sometimes allows this precisely in order to deepen the monk's humility and total reliance on God, and thus lead him to the heights of sanctity.

We must admit that it's a somewhat daunting programme that we are given here by St Benedict. And yet, it is one which leads the monk to a level of peace which surpasses the capacity of the worldly-minded. One of the greatest obstacles to real progress in the spiritual life is the cult of one's personality. It's only once you've left your ego behind that you are free to be entirely in the service of God's kingdom. It reminds one of St Ignatius' insistence upon asking for humiliations, in particular in the colloquy of the Two Standards (*Sp. Ex.* #147). Such a prayer, made consistently in the sincerity of one's heart, should lead to the seventh degree of St Benedict, for if you sincerely ask for humiliations, not only will you not be surprised when they come, but you will be happy with them, having attained such a profound level of peace that all the turmoils of the world cannot shake you.

What lesson might this hold for those who are not monks? Everyone of us is tried, put to the test, judged, and sometimes condemned, rightly or unjustly. If we have real humility, we will be able to face such trials in peace. We will speak words of peace, acknowledging that we actually deserve worse. *With them that hated peace I was peaceable,* we read in Psalm 119 (v. 9). But how is that possible? Once again, it's a matter of reminding ourselves of the profound reality of our utter dependence upon God, and of our having deserved worse treatment still because of our innumerable sins. A single mortal sin is enough to send a soul to hell for all eternity, where it would justly be tormented forever and ever. If we accept this — and it is the crystal clear teaching of the Church with all its saints and doctors — then we can accept being slighted in this life. We will find it even normal that people put us down, and we will — marvel of Divine

Grace! — be thankful to them for it, because through faith we will come to realise that they are actually serving the purpose of helping us to be free of our earthly ambitions, atone for our sins, save our soul from hell, and achieve a higher level of glory in Heaven.

"*It is good for me that thou hast humbled me*". Let's not forget those inspired words. Humiliation is good for us, because it puts us where we belong, and it prevents us from falling into the greatest of all evils, the pride that leaves us under the illusion that we are something when we are really nothing. It is only once we have come to understand and accept our nothingness that we can give ourselves over to the practice of all the good works the Lord has in store for us, and this without risk of our attributing it falsely to ourselves. God needs free men and women to do His work in the world. Humility alone really sets us free. It also prepares us for future consolation, as St Bernard comments: "When you perceive that you are being humiliated, look on it as the sign of a sure guarantee that grace is on the way. Just as the heart is puffed up with pride before its destruction, so it is humiliated before being honoured".

May the most humble Virgin, exalted now to the heights of Heaven, teach us the secret of true and perfect joy which is grounded in the truth of our nothingness before God and men.

Eighth Degree

The eighth degree of humility is that a monk do nothing except what is commended by the common rule of the monastery and the example of his superiors.

In our reflections on the first seven degrees of humility as presented in the Rule of St Benedict, we were concerned with the interior dispositions of the soul. St Benedict knows only too well that if the heart is not first converted to the Lord, the external observances will matter little. But with the eighth degree we focus on how it is that, once true humility has taken root in the soul, it manifests itself in one's demeanour and actions.

The first thing we are told is to be on our guard against making ourselves stand out. It would seem that this is one of the first pitfalls of the soul who has recently converted and is still a novice in the ways of the spirit. There is a certain tendency to believe that one is going to be better than others, and this inspires one to pose, look for an effect, present oneself as someone who has his own manner of thought and action, and which of course are better than everybody else's. If one is attentive to externals to the point of wanting to do things differently from the way they are done in the community, then it may very well be that one is more pre-occupied with self than with the Lord.

Pride has a subtle way of manifesting itself even in what are the holiest of actions. One might make a fuss about the way one pronounces certain prayers, or about certain forms of art that one esteems as particularly suited to devotion, or about a certain way of taking part in the liturgy. All that can take one away from the centre of our faith and devotion, which is a sincere longing to be like Jesus and live in His company.

Dom Bernard Maréchaux writes: "The Christian should love in all things the simplicity which excludes every pre-tence, every affectation whatever it be". This teaching comes straight from the Gospel. In the Sermon on the Mount, the Lord put us on our guard: *Take heed that you do not your justice before men, to be seen by them: otherwise you shall not have a reward of your Father who is in heaven. Therefore when thou dost an alms-deed, sound not a trumpet before thee, as the hypocrites do in the synagogues and in the streets, that they may be honoured by men. Amen I say to you, they have received their reward. But when thou dost alms, let not thy left hand know what thy right hand doth. That thy alms may be in secret, and thy Father who seeth in secret will repay thee. And when ye pray, you shall not be as the hypocrites, that love to stand and pray in the synagogues and corners of the streets, that they may be seen by men: Amen I say to you, they have received their reward. But thou when thou shalt pray, enter into thy chamber, and having shut the door, pray to thy Father in secret, and thy Father who seeth in secret will repay thee. [...] And when you fast, be not as the hypocrites, sad. For they disfigure their faces, that they may appear unto men to fast. Amen I say to you, they have received their reward. But thou, when thou fastest anoint thy head, and wash thy face; that thou appear not to men to fast, but to thy Father who is in secret: and thy Father who seeth in secret, will repay thee* (Mt 6:1-6, 16-18).

One of the first things that a newcomer notices when visiting a large monastic community is the uniformity. In the church, as he looks up towards the altar, the visitor sees rows of monks, all wearing the same choir dress, all with the same haircut, all folding their hands in the same way, all performing the same actions: standing, bowing, sitting, kneeling, etc, in unison. No one stands out. No one tries to stand out. The monastic "reflex", so to speak, the "default position", one might say, seems to be to disappear in the mass of monks, to blend in with others without being noticed, allowing Christ to take centre stage at all times.

What about those who live out there in the world, sometimes in situations where the environment is hostile to religion? What of the man whose fellow workers make fun of the faith? Or the woman who dresses with Christian modesty in a context where most others don't seem to know the meaning of the word? Or the devout person who wants to receive Holy Communion kneeling while everybody else stands? Does the 8th degree of humility mean that they should do like everybody else? Would it be virtuous to pretend not to have the faith or to dress immodestly, just because "everybody else" is doing it?

St Benedict's intention, following the command of the Lord Himself, is to ward off any desire to stand out, to blow a trumpet *as if one were better than others*. The afore-mentioned cases are all ones in which a fervent soul needs to stand out, not because of a desire to do so, but out of a necessity of conscience which makes it impossible for them to follow the crowd. However, as the Saint will make clear later on in the Rule when discussing Lenten penances, a devout soul will take care to ask the advice of a good spiritual father. This will ward off any temptations to vainglory, and will also give the soul greater incentive to persevere with keeping resolutions that may require swimming against the current. Swim against the current we must for, as G.K. Chesterton wrote: "A dead thing can go with the stream, but only a living thing can go against it." If we are unable to go against the current, chances are we are spiritually dead.

But we might ask another question: When the disciple of St Benedict resembles the crowd of people that surrounds him, does that mean his soul lowers itself to ambient mediocrities? Is the effort not to stand out and not attract attention a kind of self-condemnation to being spiritually average? Certainly not! For if nothing distinguishes such a man in the eyes of others, his interior dispositions, intentions, supernatural spirit and loving union with God, will be truly extraordinary.

We could go even further and say that, paradoxically, it is precisely one's ordinary resemblance with others which allows the soul to achieve extraordinary prowess without being noticed. Attentiveness to eccentric externals, on the other hand, deprives the soul of its spiritual energy, depth and lustre. Perhaps this is one of the reasons for the success of the monastic enterprise in history and the great influence it has had. Monks seek no influence; they attempt, rather, to disappear in the eyes of the world, and this unassuming anonymity gives them unfailing strength to undertake amazing feats, for the very simple reason that they do not feel obliged to play a role. How tiring it is to play a role! How much energy is wasted in maintaining appearances!

So, perhaps we can make a little examination of conscience based on this eighth degree of humility. How do I go about my life? Am I continually putting on masks, building up façades, passing myself off for someone I am not, but would like to be? If so, perhaps it is time I had a closer look at those long lines of hooded monks, their peace, their serenity, their joy, their amazing capacity to react to new situations. They know exactly who they are and feel no need to pretend.

In this way, I too can start to be unassuming, to not be concerned about making an impression by being different. I can discover the hidden joy that lies in being unconsidered and unknown. The bliss of humility is right there knocking at my door. Will I open and let it permeate my life?

Ninth Degree

The ninth degree of humility is that a monk restrain his tongue and keep silence, not speaking until he is questioned. For Scripture showeth that *in much talking thou canst not avoid sin* (Pr 10:19); and that *the talkative man shall not prosper on the earth* (Ps 139:12).

The Scripture verses here quoted by St Benedict are concerned with two things: avoiding sin and being guided by God in our decisions. The first citation is from the book of Proverbs (10:19) and is worth quoting in full: *In the multitude of words there shall not want sin: but he that refraineth his lips, is most wise.* The second is from Psalm 139, and refers more to the guidance that one needs in one's life.

So many sins are caused by the tongue. Hear St James: *In many things we all offend. If any man offend not in word, the same is a perfect man. He is able also with a bridle to lead about the whole body. For if we put bits into the mouths of horses, that they may obey us: and we turn about their whole body. Behold also ships, whereas they are great and are driven by strong winds, yet are they turned about with a small helm, whithersoever the force of the governor willeth. Even so the tongue is indeed a little member and boasteth great things. Behold how small a fire kindleth a great wood. And the tongue is a fire, a world of iniquity. The tongue is placed among our members, which defileth the whole body and inflameth the wheel of our nativity, being set on fire by hell. For every nature of beasts and of birds and of serpents and of the rest is tamed and hath been tamed, by the nature of man. But the tongue no man can tame, an unquiet evil, full of deadly poison. By it we bless God and the Father: and by it we curse men who are made after the likeness of God. Out of the same mouth proceedeth blessing and cursing. My brethren, these things ought not so to be. Doth a fountain send forth, out of the same hole, sweet and bitter water? Can the fig tree, my brethren, bear grapes? Or the vine, figs? So neither can the salt water yield sweet* (James 3:2-12).

St Benedict mentions silence in other passages of the Rule. There is of course a whole chapter dedicated to it (ch. 6). But in chapter 4 which treats of the "instruments of good works", he mentions: "To keep one's mouth from evil and wicked words. Not to love much speaking" (instruments 52 and 53). What is most informative is that these two are preceded by two others: "To dash down on the Rock (Christ) one's evil thoughts, the instant that they come into the heart. And to lay them open to one's spiritual father" (instruments 50 and 51). What this reveals to us is that silence of the tongue is only possible with silence of the heart, and that our fallen nature is more inclined to speak evil of others than to acknowledge our own sins.

Is it not an effect of diabolical pride that we are so prompt to speak ill of others and to proffer reprehensible words, but so terribly slow to open our mouths to our spiritual guide, to our confessor, revealing our sins and the wicked thoughts that come to us! The evil that we speak should be the evil against ourselves, acknowledging that we have deep down in us so many vices that are continually seeking to boil over and poison the world. If we have the courage and the humility to make such confession to our spiritual guide, then we will be much less prompt to speak ill of others.

The other aspect of silence implied by the second citation in the Rule is that silence not only preserves us from sin, it also allows us to discern God's will in our lives. All spiritual masters agree on this point: the first step to being able to hear God's voice in our heart is to make silence, to impose quiet on all created voices that come from without, and even on that voice within, which is the voice of the "carnal man" of whom St Paul speaks (cf. 1 Cor 3:1-3, 2 Cor 1:12), and who is regularly drawing us away from the calm, peaceful discernment of God's will.

Might we not be here in the presence of one of the major causes, not only of sin in our world, but also of the failure of so many, especially among the youth, to hear God's voice in their lives, inspiring them with generous longings to serve others and work for the salvation of souls? Is it any coincidence that the 1960's, which is the period from which the number of priestly and religious vocations dropped drastically in the universal Church, is also the period of the advent of so many devices that for the most part abolished the oases of peace? It became possible to fill the airwaves with human words and song, making it impossible for the soft breeze of the Divine Voice (see 3 Kings 19:12) and the sweet melody of the Divine Symphony to be heard.

Is there anything more indicative of this than the tragic fact that it is becoming more and more difficult to find public spaces that are not bombarded by continual noise? Or what of the youngsters who go for mountain hikes with their iPod in their ears, or the worker who cannot practice his trade without the unceasing wave of savage rhythm coming from his radio? Something is seriously wrong here, and St Benedict has an answer: silence is bred of humility.

If this analysis rings true, then silence is the first step towards retrieving a more peaceful, tranquil pace of life, devoid of senseless noise. Create spaces of silence in your life. Do not be afraid of silence. Do you know why it is that people are afraid of silence? The principal reason is that they are afraid of being alone with themselves. They do not want to face the voice of their conscience for they know it will be one of remonstrance. These two competing voices are incompatible: the voice of conscience and the voice of the world. The world seeks to drown out conscience; conscience, for its part, will have no pact with the world. You must make your choice. If you are continually listening to the world and all it has to say, chances are you are not listening to conscience. And vice versa. If you take time each day to remain in peace with the Lord, not afraid of what He might be suggesting deep down in the heart, then chances are you are on His side. The Lord is a jealous lover, He will have all of your heart, He will not settle for half, nor will He share you with the world. If you listen to God every day, you are on the right path. You will avoid sin, and you will be guided into the ways of the Spirit, who seeks your true good, your happiness on earth and your eternal salvation in Heaven.

In Psalm 139 quoted above, there is another verse worth mentioning in this context. It reads, referring to evildoers: "the labour of their lips shall overwhelm them" (Ps 139:10). The *labour* of their lips! I remember in my early years of monastic life one of the elder priests pointing out in a retreat conference that talking demands effort, not silence. Be that as it may, it is so true that so many souls lose themselves through the hard, unceasing labour of the lips. The devil is a merciless slave-driver, and life with him is more like death. Let's not exhaust ourselves with the labour of our lips.

Let us rather imitate the prophet Jeremiah, in a passage we read in Holy Week: "He shall sit solitary, and hold his peace: because he hath taken it up upon himself" (Lam 3:28). The Latin text of this verse reads: "quia levavit super se", which can also be translated: "because he lifted himself above himself". The idea is that by silence the soul lifts itself up above the petty considerations of mundane life, and also above the words of wicked or senseless people who seek to distract it and involve it in their gossip and futilities. Let us remember, in such moments, to rise above ourselves and hold our peace. If we do, we are progressing in that all-important virtue of humility, and are opening ourselves up to the Divine Peace that can resound in our hearts only inasmuch as our passions and emotions are calmed and pacified by the tranquility of union with God.

Tenth Degree

The tenth degree of humility is that he be not ready and prompt to laughter, for it is written: *The fool lifteth up his voice in laughter* (Sir 21:23).

Reading the tenth step of humility might lead some readers to the conclusion that St Benedict was just a little bit strange. Is not laughter one of the distinctive traits of humans, so much so that man has been defined as the *animal risibile*, the "animal that laughs"? To laugh is indeed proper to rational animals, for laughing requires the rational capacity to perceive what is amusing in a given situation; it demands being able to step back from the very earthly needs of creatures or their mistakes and find them somewhat comical, even when they are embarrassing. It is a wonderful thing to be able to laugh, even at oneself, and take lightly events that may throw us off.

So why does St Benedict consider that it is a mark of a very lofty sanctity to not be given over to laughter? And why, in the chapter on the "instruments of good works" (or tools of the spiritual life), does he tell us that we should not "speak vain words or such as move to laughter, nor should we love much or violent laughter" (*Rule*, ch. 4). What is it about laughter that clearly does not find favour with the patriarch of monks?

St Benedict does not proscribe laughter absolutely. He says that the monk should not be *prone to laughter*, and that he should not give himself over to *violent laughter*. Most people have direct experience of fits of laughter that are hard to control. This is healthy when kept within certain limits. It is more common among the young, and there are both psychological and physiological reasons for it. There is a certain spirit of levity that one tends to lose as one grows older.

But then there are some people who simply have no depth of soul, who laugh at everything, as if everything were a laughing matter. This is out of place. It is not rational. Such an attitude denotes a superficial soul, one that has no profundity, no maturity, little capacity to see the seriousness of life or to feel compassion for the sufferings of others. Such a lack may be culpable through want of effort to consider the real goal of life. In any case, it is not becoming of the monk who, by his profession and his very being, is a sign of the seriousness of life and the closeness of eternity. A monk should, by his very demeanour, inspire others to think of death, judgment, eternal retribution. This would not be the case if the monk were continually laughing about the oddities of life.

Another point concerns the spirit of compunction. The monk should be one whose sorrow for past sins moves him rather to be sad, not with a sadness of dejection, but with a holy sadness, like the one mentioned by St Paul to the Corinthians: *Now I am glad: not because you were made sorrowful, but because you were made sorrowful unto penance. For you were made sorrowful according to God* (2 Cor 7:9). The monk takes to heart the gravity of sin and evil in the world, and as his love for God should be great, and his desire for his neighbour's salvation intense, he considers attentively what St Benedict says concerning weeping for one's sins every day of his life, fearing judgment and hellfire, and preparing for death (Cf. *Rule*, ch. 4).

But how sad a life, some will say! There is the paradox: the monk is conscious of these austere realities, he looks them in the face, they move him to be rather pensive and prayerful, but at the same time, he never despairs of God's mercy for himself and for all repentant sinners for whom he prays, and this gives him a tranquillity of mind and heart that makes superficial mirth and laughter unnecessary and even unbecoming.

This is perhaps the place to mention Our Lord's words in the Beatitudes condoning the sadness of which we have spoken: *Blessed are ye that weep now, for you shall laugh!* (Lk 6:21). *Woe to you that now laugh: for you shall mourn and weep* (Lk 6:25). St James for his part is quite stern in his address to sinners whom he admonishes to sober up and cease living as if life were a continual party: *Draw nigh to God: and he will draw nigh to you. Cleanse your hands, ye sinners, and purify your hearts, ye double minded. Be afflicted and mourn and weep: let your laughter be turned into mourning and your joy into sorrow* (James 4:8-9).

This is reminiscent of the praise that Holy Scripture has for the woman who fears the Lord: *Strength and beauty are her clothing, and she shall laugh in the latter day* (Pr 31:25).

And the text goes on to specify: *Favour is deceitful, and beauty is vain: the woman that feareth the Lord, she shall be praised* (Pr 31:30). Can we not see here a kind of confirmation of the spiritual value of gravity and soberness? Whereas ephemeral beauty is often found together with a gusto for superficial joys and mirth-filled nights which lead to desolate mornings, we are told by the inspired author that such are not the satisfactions we should be pursuing. On the contrary, it is not appearances that should attract our attention, but realities.

Besides, does not the excessive need for entertainment in our world denote a deep sadness of the heart? Why do people have to pay someone to make them laugh? There is of course nothing wrong with watching a comedy every now and then — assuming it's morally decent —, but when one starts to rely on it as a drug, there is something seriously wrong, a spiritual cancer of sorts that will not allow one to be at peace, and prevents the repose of the mind and heart. Just as some seek to drown their sorrow — or their bad conscience — in drugs, alcohol, the pleasures of the flesh or excessive use of media, so do some with an unhealthy and excessive recourse to entertainment. *It is better to go to the house of mourning than to the house of feasting, for that is the end of every man, and the living should take it to heart. Sorrow is better than laughter, because when the face is sad the heart grows wiser. The heart of the wise is in the house of mourning, but the heart of fools is in the house of mirth* (Ecc 7:2-4). Better to enjoy the pure, calm, fulfilling joys of reading good, solid books, and spending more time in prayer, than the ephemeral thrills which distract the soul and leave it barren and fitful.

One last consideration. St Thomas Aquinas, after Aristotle, tells us that there is virtue called *eutrapelia*, which can be defined as "pleasantness in conversation" (cf. Ia-IIae, q. 60, a. 5). It is the golden mean between boorishness and buffoonery. It is a virtue which makes social life pleasant. However, as with every virtue, it is easy to exceed on one side or the other. The boisterous laughter proscribed by St Benedict would fall under the vice of buffoonery. So what are we to say of the habit of poking inoffensive jokes at others, which — so we think — are as funny for them as for ourselves? Caution: someone is always the butt of a joke, and the one who tells it more often than not subconsciously thinks himself better than the one he is making fun of. This is precisely one of the reasons for which we are at a lofty degree of humility here: the truly humble soul rarely pokes fun, and only when confident that the other is himself humble enough for it to do him some good.

So once again, we see that humility is a virtue which resolves many problems. With it, one stands on solid ground and knows how to adapt oneself to every situation. Humble souls know that everything does not depend on them; humble souls are not egocentric; humble souls rest in peace with the sure knowledge that, come what may, we are in the hands of God: and that gives a peaceful reassurance that makes worldly distractions, for the most part, unnecessary and even undesirable.

Far from being out of touch with reality, St Benedict reveals himself to be a fine connoisseur of humanity, an adroit guide along the path to happiness. He has a lot to teach, and not only to monks. Everyone can learn from his wisdom.

Eleventh Degree

The eleventh degree of humility is that a monk, when he speaks, do so gently and without laughter, humbly and seriously, in few and sensible words, and without clamour. It is written: *A wise man is known by the fewness of his words**.

In the ninth degree we meditated on silence and saw how humility leads to silence. A monk, says St Benedict, need not speak until he is questioned. Here in degree eleven, he seeks to make it clear that even when questioned or bound to speak for any other reason, the monk does so with characteristic parsimony. Instead of a river of words, a gentle trickle should flow from his mouth, something like a few drops of precious liquor, all the more precious in that it is rare.

---

*   This citation is not from Holy Scripture, but from the Sentences of Sextus, a collection of sayings by an unknown Greek philosopher and latinised by Rufinus.

It is told that there was once a well-known priest who went to a monastery for a day of retreat. Upon his arrival, the monk guest master led him to his room and ventured a question or two about the priest's activities which were making the headlines. To his dismay, the monk got this response: "Brother, you get payed to shut your mouth, so shut it!" This rather abrupt manner of putting the monk in his place is an illustration of what the monk should not do, that is, be curious about the sayings and doings of others.

This control over the tongue demands effort. Learning to keep silence is one thing. Learning to use few words to say what needs to be said is another, in a way harder. We have all experienced that there are certain things it is easier to abstain from completely rather than use sparingly. This is perhaps the reason that St Benedict considers it to be a higher form of humility.

When the monk speaks, the words that come forth should have been matured in long prayer and contemplation. If they are, they need not be many. This demands lengthy, attentive listening to God's word, it involves convincing oneself that, in the end, all that really matters is what God has to say. God, writes St John of the Cross, has spoken once, through His Word, and in that Word He has said everything we need to know about Him. In a similar way, the monk should learn how to weigh his words, to limit them to those that are essential, words that will foster charity and the other virtues, words that will edify and console hearts. This also implies coming to a deeper appreciation for the power of the spoken word. Speech is an extraordinary gift God has given to us, and we too often take it for granted. A bit more contemplation will teach us the value of words.

St Benedict mentions not only the fewness of words, but also their manner. There are modes of speech that do not befit the monk. A boisterous, noisy monk would strike one as being out of place. A monk who would be prone to poke fun or to speak lightly of people and things would seem unfit for the monastic life.

So what application can we make to those who are not monks? How can the laity implement this degree without appearing to be taciturn or unsociable? For sure, there are certain attitudes that are proper in a monastery, that would be out of place elsewhere.

I would suggest one good way of going about it would be to try to convince oneself that what we have to say might not be *that* important, and that what others have to say might be just as important, if not more so. Apart from being often true, it is a sobering thought, likely to help us bite our tongue when we should. How many regretted words would be avoided if we would only take the advice given here by the patriarch of monks?

The monk may "get paid to shut his mouth", but everyone will be all the richer for learning the secret of silence and fewness of words. St Benedict would probably concur with that saying of the celebrity priest, at least up to a certain point. However, there is a lot more to it than that. Silence in the monastery is silence that is creative. The monk does not hold his peace for money, but he imposes silence on created tongues, his own included, to give optimal resonance to the Word of God. God speaks to us through Holy Scripture and therefore through the Sacred Liturgy which the monk is privileged to celebrate throughout the day. As he chants the office, the monk speaks to God using God's words and, by doing so, he is allowing God to reach the ears of those who are present. But we can go further and say that the recitation or the chant of the office gives God's word a space to resonate spiritually in the world, in such a way that, even though few be there physically present, the Word is heard, and going forth from the bosom of God, through the monk's mouth, it fecundates the entire world, as it were, preparing an abundant harvest.

God also speaks to us through events, and through other people. The monk who has grown accustomed to seeing and hearing God in all things will ever be attentive to what others might say to him or ask of him. It is precisely because of his efforts to hear God that, when required to speak, the monks does so "gently and without laughter, humbly and seriously, in few and sensible words, and without clamour".

The monk's model in this attitude is first and foremost Our Blessed Lady who, in many respects, we could call the first "nun". Her words as recorded in Scripture are brief. She speaks only seven times, and if we leave aside the Magnificat, her hymn of praise, her words are always very brief. She does not waste time speaking about others; she has her duties, and she fulfils them to perfection. She is conscious that an abundance of words leads into many sins of the tongue. Besides, she is too busy listening to the Eternal Word. If she merited to receive Him into her flesh, it was because she had first received Him in the silent prayer of her heart.

St Elisabeth of the Trinity, in her extraordinarily beautiful prayer to the Trinity, expresses herself this way: "O Eternal Word, Utterance of my God! I yearn to spend my life in listening to Thee, to become wholly docile, that I may learn all from Thee. Then, through all nights, all emptiness, all helplessness, I long to gaze on Thee always and to dwell beneath Thy lustrous beams. O my beloved Star! So fascinate me that I may never again withdraw from Thy radiance!"

Twelfth Degree

The twelfth degree of humility is that a monk should not only be humble of heart, but should also in his behaviour always manifest his humility to those who look upon him. That is to say, that whether he is at the Work of God, in the oratory, in the monastery, in the garden, on the road, in the fields, or anywhere else, and whether sitting, walking or standing, he should always have his head bowed and his eyes downcast, pondering always the guilt of his sins, and considering that he is about to be brought before the dread judgment seat of God. Let him constantly say in his heart what was said with downcast eyes by the publican in the Gospel: *Lord, I a sinner am not worthy to raise mine eyes to heaven* (Lk 18:13); and again with the prophet: *I am bowed down and humbled on every side* (cf. Ps 37:7; Ps 118:107).

At last we have arrived at the summit of the virtue of humility, the ladder which one takes downward, but which is then lifted up by God according to the measure of one's progress. Having arrived at the most profound humility, it has become second nature; the monk, as by instinct, appears humble. He not only *is* humble, he *looks* humble. "He should always have his head bowed and his eyes downcast". I'm not sure what modern psychologists would say about that. It sounds something like an inferiority complex. Perhaps we are here at one of those attitudes that are inspired solely by faith and become incomprehensible without it. One is reminded of those extremely counter-cultural attitudes that were inspired by Our Lords's words, such as: "He that loveth father or mother more than me, is not worthy of me…" (Mt 10:37); "If any man come to me, and hate not his father, and mother, and wife, and children, and brethren, and sisters, yea and his own life also, he cannot be my disciple" (Lk 14:26). Those words demand total adherence to Christ at the risk of losing everything else. No human affections stand when it is a matter of fidelity to God.

Here we have a similar attitude. The monk who has achieved the summit of humility and perfection reflects in everything he says and does the attitude of one who is about to be judged by God for his sins. In chapter 4 of the Rule, St Benedict counts among the instruments of good works "to weep everyday for the sins of one's life". This is for monks, monks who have spent years, decades even, praying, working, serving the Lord. How is this possible?

It is possible only when, through faith, one has come to realise the gravity of sin, the deleterious effect it has on self and on the whole world. But in the mind of St Benedict this twelfth degree is followed without delay by the casting out of fear and the delight of virtue. In other words, the deeper you go down into the valley of humility, the more you are conscious of the gravity of sin, of *your* sins, the more you expose yourself to the superabundant joy of the Holy Spirit that is made manifest in one who has been fully purified.

It might help to compare this with a trampoline. The lower you descend into the valley of your wretchedness, the higher you are projected into the joy of God. The longer and harder you accept to look your sinfulness straight in the face, the higher chance you have of actually discovering, even in this life, the sweet joy of the Divine embrace. We could also say that, if St Benedict's analysis is trustworthy – and who would make bold to doubt it? –, unless you accept to go down that path, to sink into the mire of your ontological nothingness and your spiritual insignificance, you will never attain to that state in which you run with joy on the way of the commandments. Here we see how the modern current that consists in denying sin or denying that it is really serious and can separate from God for eternity, is actually a road block to peace and serenity in this life as it is a falsehood that derails from the path that leads to Heaven.

So how does one go about obtaining that level of humility? The first step is to ask for the grace to throw off the mask of our self-justification, to step on our pride and acknowledge our failings. To achieve this, I know of no better aid than St Ignatius' first week, in which, by overlapping layers of contemplation, the focus of our mind and heart zooms into sin and its consequences, showing us its devastating effects on our lives. One of the high points of that journey is the triple colloquy of the Third Exercise. It goes like this:

"The first colloquy will be with our Blessed Lady, that she may obtain grace for me from her Son and Lord for three favours: 1. A deep knowledge of my sins and a feeling of abhorrence for them; 2. An understanding of the disorder of my actions, that filled with horror of them, I may amend my life and put it in order; 3. A knowledge of the world, that filled with horror, I may put away from me all that is worldly and vain. Then I will say a *Hail Mary.* I will make the same petitions to her Son that He may obtain these graces from the Father for me. After that I will say *Soul of Christ.* I will make the same requests of the Father that He Himself, the eternal Lord, may grant them to me. Then I will close with the *Our Father*" (*Sp. Ex.* # 63).

This little prayer is a masterpiece. Like every masterpiece, a quick glance does not suffice to take it all in. Time is needed to delve into it, and let the reality transform us. Each part of the prayer includes a request that our minds be enlightened and our heart filled with horror and disgust. First, there are our sins, then there are the internal causes of our sins, that is to say our own passions and pride, finally the external causes of our sins, namely the influence of the world. The repetition of this prayer has a beneficial and pacifying effect; it leads firmly but gently to the truth; we see things as they are, and nowhere does a human being find peace as he does in the truth. Never forget: the devil is allergic to reality and he seeks to infect us all with that rebellion.

At the end we see how the attitude of head bowed and eyes lowered is fully compatible with true joy in the Holy Spirit. The monastic ideal once again reveals itself as having a lot to say to our contemporaries. The world says, "Affirm yourself, defend your rights, lift up your head and impose upon others," and it ends up creating conflicts and destabilising people. St Benedict says, "Bow your head, humble yourself, acknowledge the rights of God and others, put yourself in the last place," and he makes men and women who are serene, joyful, full of the Holy Spirit, the exact kind of person we need to build a world of true justice and harmony. The paradox is ever there. "Everyone that exalteth himself shall be humbled, and he that humbleth himself shall be exalted" (Lk 18:14).

Conclusion

Then, when all these degrees of humility have been climbed, the monk will presently come to that perfect love of God which casts out all fear (cf. 1 Jn 4:18); whereby he will begin to observe without labour, as though naturally and by habit, all those precepts which formerly he did not observe without fear: no longer for fear of hell, but for love of Christ and through good habit and delight in virtue. And this will the Lord deign to show forth by the power of His Spirit in His workman now cleansed from vice and from sin.

In conclusion of the twelve degrees, St Benedict feels the need to remind us with Holy Scripture that "the fear of the Lord is the beginning of wisdom" (Ps 110:10). The fear of the Lord moves the sinner to conversion; it moves the negligent soul to greater fervour. It is a good thing. This has been admirably expressed by St Ignatius: "Though the zealous service of God our Lord out of pure love should be esteemed above all, we ought also to praise highly the fear of the Divine Majesty. For not only filial fear but also servile fear is pious and very holy. When nothing higher or more useful is attained, it is very helpful for rising from mortal sin, and once this is accomplished, one may easily advance to filial fear, which is wholly pleasing and agreeable to God our Lord since it is inseparably associated with the love of Him" (Sp. Ex. # 370).

In the face of those who would want us to think that serving God out of fear of punishment is a bad thing, the saints show us that, on the contrary, a truly Christian life begins with fear. "*With fear and trembling work out your salvation*," wrote St Paul (Ph 2:12). But that fear, which can be somewhat servile at the start, is destined to be transformed into filial fear, that which a loving child has of not offending his parents, not for fear of punishment but simply because he does not want to offend its beloved parents. Better still, it is the spousal fear, that of the one who, because of its love, would never hurt its wedded spouse.

St Benedict, following St John, tells us that perfect love casts out fear, and that it is present when one has attained to the deepest humility. What does it mean? Perfect humility and perfect love arise together. "It is proper to love to lower itself", as St Therese of Lisieux wrote. If one has been fully emptied of all ambition and is accepting of the last place, fear no longer plays a vital role, and love takes command. Fear, of course, is one of the Gifts of the Holy Spirit which every soul in the state of grace possesses, and as such it remains, but it is no longer the principle motive, being superseded by a great love for God. At this level, even though fear will "kick in" at certain moments of particularly serious temptation, love for Christ has led to developing good habits of all the virtues, which no longer, at least habitually, need to be commanded by fear of God's punishment. Then becomes true the word of St Augustine: "Love, and do as you please", for your love will be so great that you would never even entertain a thought of offending God or neighbour.

Such is the perfection to which we are called and at which we will arrive if we persevere humbly seeking God's will.

Appendix
Prayers for Humility

Thomas à Kempis
Imitation of Christ, Book 3, ch. 8

I will speak unto my Lord who am but dust and ashes (cf. Gn 18:27). If I count myself more, behold Thou standest against me, and my iniquities bear true testimony, and I cannot gainsay it. But if I abase myself, and bring myself to nought, and shrink from all self-esteem, and grind myself to dust, which I am, Thy grace will be favourable unto me, and Thy light will be near unto my heart; and all self-esteem, how little soever it be, shall be swallowed up in the depths of my nothingness, and shall perish for ever.

There Thou showest to me myself, what I am, what I was, and whither I have come: so foolish was I and ignorant (cf. Ps 72:22). If I am left to myself, behold I am nothing, I am all weakness; but if suddenly Thou look upon me, immediately I am made strong, and filled with new joy. And it is great marvel that I am so suddenly lifted up, and so graciously embraced by Thee, since I am always being carried to the deep by my own weight.

This is the doing of Thy love which freely goeth before me and succoureth me in so many necessities, which guardeth me also in great dangers and snatcheth me, as I may truly say, from innumerable evils. For verily, by loving myself amiss, I lost myself, and by seeking and sincerely loving Thee alone, I found both myself and Thee, and through love I have brought myself to yet deeper nothingness: because Thou, O most sweet Lord, dealest with me beyond all merit, and above all which I dare ask or think.

Blessed be Thou, O my God, because though I be unworthy of all Thy benefits, Thy bountiful and infinite goodness never ceaseth to do good even to ingrates and to those who are turned far from Thee. Turn Thou us unto Thyself, that we may be grateful, humble, and godly, for Thou art our salvation, our courage, and our strength (cf. Ps 61:8).,h

St Therese of Lisieux
From a letter dated 16 July 1897

O Jesus! When Thou wert a Pilgrim on earth, Thou didst say: "Learn of Me for I am meek and humble of heart and you will find rest for your souls." O Mighty Monarch of Heaven, yes, my soul finds rest in seeing Thee, clothed in the form and nature of a slave, humbling Thyself to wash the feet of Thine apostles. I recall Thy words that teach me how to practice humility: "I have given you an example so that you may do what I have done. The disciple is no greater than the Master ... If you understand this, happy are you if you put them into practice." Lord, I do understand these words that came from Thy gentle and humble heart and I want to practice them with the help of Thy grace.

I beg Thee, my Divine Jesus, to send me a humiliation whenever I try to set myself above others. I know, O my God, that Thou dost humble the proud soul but to the one who humbles one's self Thou dost give an eternity of glory. So I want to put myself in the last rank and to share Thy humiliations so as "to have a share with Thee" in the kingdom of Heaven. But, Thou dost know my weakness, Lord. Every morning I make a resolution to practice humility and in the evening I recognise that I have committed again many faults of pride. At this I am tempted to become discouraged but I know that discouragement is also pride. Therefore, O my God, I want to base my hope in Thee alone. Since Thou canst do everything, deign to bring to birth in my soul the virtue I desire. To obtain this grace of Thine infinite mercy I will very often repeat: "O Jesus, gentle and humble of heart, make my heart like Thine!"

Rafael Cardinal Merry del Val (1865-1930)
Secretary of State of Pope St Pius X
Litany of Humility

Lord Jesus, meek and humble of heart, *Hear me.*
From the desire of being esteemed, *Deliver me, Jesus.*
From the desire of being loved, *Deliver me, Jesus.*
From the desire of being extolled, *Deliver me, Jesus.*
From the desire of being honoured, *Deliver me, Jesus.*
From the desire of being praised, *Deliver me, Jesus.*
From the desire of being preferred to others, *Deliver me, Jesus.*
From the desire of being consulted, *Deliver me, Jesus.*
From the desire of being approved, *Deliver me, Jesus.*
From the fear of being humiliated, *Deliver me, Jesus.*
From the fear of being despised, *Deliver me, Jesus.*
From the fear of suffering rebukes, *Deliver me, Jesus.*
From the fear of being calumniated, *Deliver me, Jesus.*
From the fear of being forgotten, *Deliver me, Jesus.*
From the fear of being ridiculed, *Deliver me, Jesus.*
From the fear of being wronged, *Deliver me, Jesus.*
From the fear of being suspected, *Deliver me, Jesus.*
That others may be loved more than I, *Jesus, grant me the grace to desire it.*
That others may be esteemed more than I, *Jesus, grant me the grace to desire it.*
That, in the opinion of the world, others may increase and I may decrease, *Jesus, grant me the grace to desire it.*
That others may be chosen and I set aside, *Jesus, grant me the grace to desire it.*
That others may be praised and I unnoticed, *Jesus, grant me the grace to desire it.*

That others may be preferred to me in everything, *Jesus, grant me the grace to desire it.*

That others may become holier than I, provided that I may become as holy as I should, *Jesus, grant me the grace to desire it.*